Navigating the Transportation Industry: A Guide to Creating a Business Plan

Content

Chapter 1. *Introduction*

Introduction: Understanding the Transportation Industry

Welcome to the world of transportation! As you embark on your journey to create a successful business plan for your transportation company, it's essential to have a comprehensive understanding of the industry. The transportation industry is vast and encompasses various modes of transportation, including ground, air, water, and rail.

The transportation sector is crucial for economic growth and plays a vital role in connecting businesses and people globally. The industry is constantly evolving, and staying abreast of the latest trends and advancements is crucial for success. In this chapter, we'll delve into the basics of the transportation industry, its importance, and the various types of transportation companies.

The Importance of the Transportation Industry

The transportation industry is vital to our daily lives and has far-reaching impacts on society and the economy. Without efficient transportation systems, it would be difficult to move goods, people, and information from one place to another. The industry plays a crucial role in facilitating trade, promoting economic growth, and connecting businesses and communities.

Additionally, transportation has significant environmental impacts, and as such, companies in the industry must take steps to minimize their environmental footprint. Companies are also expected to provide safe, reliable, and affordable transportation services, ensuring that everyone can access the benefits that transportation provides.

Types of Transportation Companies

The transportation industry encompasses a wide range of companies, each offering different services. Some of the most common types of transportation companies include:

- Ground transportation: This type of transportation encompasses all forms of ground transportation, including trucks, buses, and taxis. Ground transportation companies offer services such as package delivery, passenger transportation, and freight transportation.

- Air transportation: Air transportation companies operate planes and helicopters, providing services such as passenger transportation, air cargo, and air ambulance services.

- Water transportation: Water transportation companies operate ships and boats, providing services such as freight transportation, passenger transportation, and tourism.

- Rail transportation: Rail transportation companies operate trains and offer services such as passenger transportation, freight transportation, and tourism.

In conclusion, the transportation industry is vast and encompasses various types of transportation companies. Understanding the importance of the industry and the different types of companies within it is crucial for developing a successful business plan. In the chapters ahead, we'll delve deeper into the specifics of creating a business plan for your transportation company, including market analysis, competition, finances, and marketing. Get ready to take the first step towards building a successful transportation company!

Chapter 2. *Market Analysis: Assessing the Industry and Competition*

Market analysis is a critical component of creating a business plan for your transportation company. The market analysis helps you understand the industry, identify opportunities, and assess your competition. This chapter will guide you through the process of conducting a market analysis, including steps to identify industry trends, assess market size and growth, and analyze your competition.

Understanding Industry Trends

The transportation industry is constantly evolving, and it's essential to keep abreast of the latest trends and advancements. Industry trends can include technological innovations, changes in consumer behavior, and regulatory developments. Staying up-to-date on industry trends can help you identify new market opportunities and develop strategies to stay ahead of the competition.

To conduct a market analysis, you'll need to gather information on the industry and its trends. Some useful sources of information include industry reports, trade associations, government agencies, and news articles.

Assessing Market Size and Growth

Once you have a good understanding of the industry, you'll need to assess the size and growth of the market. Market size refers to the total number of customers in the market, while market growth refers to the rate at which the market is expanding.

Market size and growth information can be found through market research reports, government agencies, and trade associations. This information will help you determine the potential size of the market for your transportation company and whether there are opportunities for growth.

Analyzing Your Competition

In the transportation industry, competition is fierce, and it's essential to understand who your competitors are and what they offer. This information will help you develop strategies to differentiate your company from the competition and position yourself in the market.

To analyze your competition, you'll need to gather information on their offerings, market share, strengths, and weaknesses. This information can be found through market research reports, government agencies, and trade associations. Additionally, you can conduct primary research by speaking with customers and conducting surveys.

In conclusion, market analysis is a crucial component of creating a business plan for your transportation company. By understanding industry trends, assessing market size and growth, and analyzing your competition, you'll be better equipped to develop strategies to succeed in the market. In the next chapter, we'll delve into developing your transportation company's marketing strategies.

write style human and friendly a full chapter on "Marketing Strategies: Reaching Your Target Market", make it detailed

Marketing Strategies: Reaching Your Target Market

Once you have completed your market analysis, it's time to turn your attention to developing a marketing strategy to reach your target market. A marketing strategy is a plan that outlines how you will communicate with potential customers, promote your transportation services, and reach your business goals.

Defining Your Target Market

The first step in developing a marketing strategy is to identify your target market. A target market is a specific group of customers that your transportation services are aimed at. The more specific you can be about your target market, the better equipped you will be to reach them effectively.

To identify your target market, consider factors such as demographics, location, income level, and buying behavior. This information can be found through market research reports, customer surveys, and demographic data.

Developing a Unique Value Proposition

Once you have identified your target market, it's time to develop a unique value proposition. A value proposition is a statement that explains the benefits of your transportation services and what sets them apart from the competition.

A strong value proposition will help you communicate the unique benefits of your transportation services to your target market, making it easier to attract and retain customers. To develop a value proposition, consider the following:

- What benefits do your transportation services offer that are different from the competition?

- How do your transportation services meet the needs of your target market?

- What sets your transportation services apart from the competition?

Promoting Your Transportation Services

Once you have a unique value proposition, it's time to start promoting your transportation services. There are several marketing channels you can use to reach your target market, including:

- Website: Your website should be professional, easy to navigate, and provide information on your transportation services and how to book them.

- Social media: Social media is a powerful tool for promoting your transportation services and connecting with your target market.

- Email marketing: Email marketing allows you to reach your target market directly with promotions and updates on your transportation services.

- Referral marketing: Encourage satisfied customers to refer friends and family to your transportation services.

- Advertising: Advertise your transportation services in relevant magazines, newspapers, and online platforms.

In conclusion, developing a marketing strategy is an essential component of creating a business plan for your transportation company. By identifying your target market, developing a unique value proposition, and promoting your transportation services, you'll be better equipped to reach your target market and achieve your business goals. In the next chapter, we'll delve into the financial aspects of starting a transportation company, including budgeting, pricing, and financial projections.

 # *Defining Your Business: Creating a Unique Identity*

Creating a unique identity for your transportation company is essential for differentiating yourself from the competition and building a strong brand. A well-defined brand identity will help you communicate what your transportation company stands for and what makes it special.

Developing Your Brand Name

The first step in creating a unique identity for your transportation company is to develop a brand name. A brand name is the name that represents your transportation services and sets you apart from the competition.

When developing a brand name, consider the following:

- Make it memorable: Choose a name that is easy to remember and will stick in customers' minds.

- Make it descriptive: A descriptive name can help customers understand what your transportation services are all about.

- Make it unique: Avoid names that are too similar to your competition or that are difficult to spell or pronounce.

Creating a Logo and Brand Identity

Once you have developed a brand name, it's time to create a logo and brand identity. A logo is a visual representation of your transportation company and is an essential component of your brand identity. Your logo should be simple, memorable, and recognizable, and it should represent the values and mission of your transportation company.

In addition to a logo, you'll also need to develop a brand identity, including a color palette, font, and overall visual style. These elements should be consistent across all of your marketing materials and should reflect the personality and values of your transportation company.

Building a Brand Culture

Your brand identity goes beyond just your logo and visual elements. Building a brand culture involves creating a consistent brand experience for your customers, from the way your employees interact with customers to the way your vehicles are maintained.

Creating a brand culture involves the following steps:

- Define your values and mission: What is your transportation company all about? What values and principles guide your business?

- Communicate your values and mission: Make sure your employees and customers understand your values and mission and how they are reflected in your transportation services.

- Create a consistent customer experience: Make sure the customer experience is consistent across all aspects of your transportation services, from booking to arrival.

- Train your employees: Train your employees to embody your values and mission and to deliver a consistent brand experience.

In conclusion, defining your business and creating a unique identity is an essential component of creating a business plan for your transportation company. By developing a brand name, creating a logo and brand identity, and building a brand culture, you'll be better equipped to differentiate your transportation company from the competition and build a strong brand. In the next chapter, we'll delve into the operational aspects of starting a transportation company, including fleet management, safety and security, and customer service.

Chapter 4. *Service Offerings: Identifying What You Can Provide*

When starting a transportation business, it's important to identify the types of services you can offer and what sets your business apart from the competition. This chapter will guide you through the process of defining your service offerings and creating a unique value proposition.

Identifying Your Niche

The first step in defining your service offerings is to identify your niche. This is the specific area of the transportation industry that your business will focus on. For example, you might specialize in transportation for tourists, transportation for corporate events, or transportation for seniors.

When identifying your niche, consider the following:

- What are your skills and experience? What types of transportation services do you feel most confident providing?

- What is the demand for your services? Is there a market for your niche in your area?

- What is your competition like? What types of transportation services are they offering and how can you differentiate yourself?

Defining Your Service Offerings

Once you've identified your niche, you'll need to define your service offerings. This includes identifying the types of transportation services you'll provide, the vehicles you'll use, and the types of customers you'll serve.

Consider the following when defining your service offerings:

- Types of transportation services: Will you offer airport transportation, city tours, or charter services?

- Vehicles: What types of vehicles will you use, such as buses, vans, or limousines?

- Customer types: Who will your target customers be, such as tourists, corporate clients, or seniors?

Creating a Unique Value Proposition

Your service offerings and niche will help you create a unique value proposition for your transportation business. A unique value proposition is a statement that defines what sets your business apart from the competition and what benefits customers can expect from your services.

When creating your unique value proposition, consider the following:

- What are the unique features of your transportation services?

- What are the benefits of your transportation services for customers?

- How do your transportation services meet the needs of your target customers?

In conclusion, defining your service offerings and creating a unique value proposition is an important component of creating a business plan for your transportation company. By identifying your niche, defining your service offerings, and creating a unique value proposition, you'll be better equipped to differentiate your transportation company from the competition and build a successful business. In the next chapter, we'll discuss the financial aspects of starting a transportation company, including start-up costs, pricing strategies, and budgeting.

Chapter 5. *Financial Projections: Estimating Your Costs and Earnings*

When starting a transportation business, it's important to understand the financial aspects of your company. This chapter will guide you through the process of estimating your costs and earnings, and creating financial projections for your business.

Start-Up Costs

The first step in creating financial projections is to estimate your start-up costs. This includes the costs of equipment, supplies, and licensing fees. When estimating your start-up costs, consider the following:

- Equipment costs: What types of vehicles will you need, and how much will they cost to purchase or lease?

- Supplies costs: What types of supplies will you need, such as fuel, maintenance supplies, and marketing materials?

- Licensing fees: What types of licenses will you need, and how much will they cost?

Operating Costs

Once you've estimated your start-up costs, you'll need to estimate your operating costs. These are the costs of running your business on a day-to-day basis, such as fuel costs, maintenance costs, and labor costs. When estimating your operating costs, consider the following:

- Fuel costs: How much fuel will you need to purchase each month, and at what cost?

- Maintenance costs: What types of maintenance will you need to perform on your vehicles, and how much will they cost?

- Labor costs: How many employees will you need, and what will their salaries be?

Revenue Projections

After estimating your costs, you'll need to estimate your revenue projections. This includes estimating how much money you'll earn from your transportation services, and how much profit you'll make. When estimating your revenue projections, consider the following:

- Pricing strategies: How much will you charge for your transportation services, and what pricing strategies will you use?

- Market demand: How much demand is there for your transportation services in your area?

- Competition: What are the prices of your competition, and how can you differentiate yourself from them?

In conclusion, understanding the financial aspects of your transportation business is critical to its success. By estimating your start-up costs, operating costs, and revenue projections, you'll be better equipped to create a budget for your company and make informed decisions about its future. In the next chapter, we'll discuss the importance of marketing and advertising for your transportation company, and how to create a marketing plan that will help you reach your target customers.

Chapter 6. Marketing Strategy: Attracting Customers and Building Brand Awareness

As a transportation business, attracting customers and building brand awareness are key to your success. This chapter will guide you through the process of creating a marketing strategy that will help you reach your target customers and build a strong brand image.

Define Your Target Market

The first step in creating a marketing strategy is to define your target market. Who are your customers, and what are their needs and preferences? When defining your target market, consider the following:

- Demographic information: What is the age, gender, income, and education level of your target market?

- Geographic information: Where do your target customers live and work?

- Psychographic information: What are their interests, values, and lifestyle?

Develop Your Unique Selling Proposition (USP)

Once you've defined your target market, the next step is to develop your unique selling proposition (USP). What makes your transportation business unique and different from your competition? When developing your USP, consider the following:

- Quality of service: How will you provide a better quality of service than your competition?

- Cost: How will you provide a more affordable cost than your competition?

- Convenience: How will you provide a more convenient transportation service than your competition?

Marketing Mix

The marketing mix refers to the four elements of marketing: product, price, place, and promotion. In the context of your transportation business, the marketing mix may look like this:

- Product: Your transportation services.

- Price: The cost of your transportation services.

- Place: The locations where your transportation services are available.

- Promotion: The methods you'll use to promote your transportation services, such as advertising, word-of-mouth, and public relations.

When creating your marketing mix, consider how each element will help you reach your target customers and build brand awareness. For example, if your target market is cost-conscious, you may want to focus on promoting your affordable prices.

Marketing Budget

Finally, you'll need to create a marketing budget. How much money will you allocate for marketing and advertising each month or year? When creating your marketing budget, consider the following:

- Cost of advertising: How much will you spend on advertising, such as print, online, and radio ads?

- Cost of public relations: How much will you spend on public relations, such as press releases and media outreach?

- Cost of promotional materials: How much will you spend on promotional materials, such as flyers, brochures, and business cards?

In conclusion, creating a marketing strategy is critical to the success of your transportation business. By defining your target market, developing your unique selling proposition, creating a marketing mix, and creating a marketing budget, you'll be better equipped to reach your target customers and build brand awareness. In the next chapter, we'll discuss the importance of a strong brand image, and how to create a brand that represents your transportation business.

Chapter 7.   **Operations and Logistics: Planning the Execution of Services**

Operations and logistics are the backbone of any transportation business. This chapter will guide you through the process of planning and executing your transportation services, from start to finish.

Define Your Service Offerings

The first step in planning your operations and logistics is to define your service offerings. What transportation services will you provide, and to whom? When defining your service offerings, consider the following:

- Type of transportation: Will you provide car, truck, bus, or bike transportation?

- Route: Will you provide transportation services within a specific geographic area, or across multiple locations?

- Schedule: Will you provide transportation services on a set schedule, or on demand?

- Customer: Who are your customers, and what are their transportation needs and preferences?

Create a Service Delivery Plan

Once you've defined your service offerings, the next step is to create a service delivery plan. How will you execute your transportation services, from start to finish? When creating your service delivery plan, consider the following:

- Vehicles: What vehicles will you use to provide your transportation services?

- Staff: Who will drive the vehicles, and what qualifications and experience do they need?

- Equipment: What equipment will you need to provide your transportation services, such as GPS, radios, and communication devices?

- Procedures: What procedures will you follow to ensure the quality of your transportation services, such as vehicle maintenance, driver training, and customer feedback?

Establish Logistics and Dispatch Operations

In addition to your service delivery plan, you'll also need to establish logistics and dispatch operations. Logistics refers to the planning and management of the physical movement of goods, people, and vehicles. Dispatch operations refer to the coordination of transportation services in real-time, based on customer demand and availability. When establishing your logistics and dispatch operations, consider the following:

- Routes: What routes will you use to provide your transportation services, and how will you optimize your routes for efficiency and cost savings?

- Dispatch software: What dispatch software will you use to manage your transportation services, and how will you integrate it with your existing systems?

- Communication: How will you communicate with your drivers, customers, and support staff, and what processes and procedures will you follow?

In conclusion, operations and logistics are critical to the success of your transportation business. By defining your service offerings, creating a service delivery plan, and establishing logistics and dispatch operations, you'll be better equipped to plan and execute your transportation services with confidence. In the next chapter, we'll discuss the importance of safety, compliance, and insurance, and how to protect your transportation business from potential risks and liabilities.

Chapter 8. Legal and Regulatory Requirements: Navigating Rules and Regulations

Starting a transportation business involves a variety of legal and regulatory requirements, including licenses, permits, insurance, and more. This chapter will guide you through the process of navigating the rules and regulations that apply to your transportation business, and help you ensure that you're in compliance with all applicable laws and regulations.

Understand the Laws and Regulations that Apply to Your Business

The first step in navigating the legal and regulatory requirements of your transportation business is to understand the laws and regulations that apply. Some of the key laws and regulations that apply to transportation businesses include:

- Federal Motor Carrier Safety Administration (FMCSA) regulations: The FMCSA sets safety standards and regulations for commercial motor carriers, including driver qualifications, vehicle maintenance, and recordkeeping.

- Department of Transportation (DOT) regulations: The DOT sets regulations for transportation businesses, including licensing, insurance, and inspection requirements.

- State regulations: Each state has its own set of regulations that apply to transportation businesses, including licensing, insurance, and operational requirements.

Obtain the Required Licenses and Permits

Once you understand the laws and regulations that apply to your transportation business, the next step is to obtain the required licenses and permits. Some of the licenses and permits you may need include:

- DOT number: A DOT number is a unique identifier that the DOT assigns to transportation businesses.

- Operating authority: Operating authority is the authority granted by the DOT to operate a transportation business.

- State licenses: Depending on your state, you may need to obtain a state license to operate a transportation business, such as a commercial driver's license (CDL) or a business license.

Comply with Insurance Requirements

Insurance is another important legal and regulatory requirement for transportation businesses. You'll need to comply with both federal and state insurance requirements, which may include:

- Liability insurance: Liability insurance covers the costs of damages or injuries that you may cause to others while operating your transportation business.

- Workers' compensation insurance: Workers' compensation insurance covers the costs of injuries or illnesses that your employees may suffer while working for your transportation business.

Ensure Compliance with Safety and Environmental Regulations

In addition to the other legal and regulatory requirements, transportation businesses must also comply with safety and environmental regulations. Some of the key safety and environmental regulations that apply to transportation businesses include:

- Hours of service regulations: Hours of service regulations set limits on the number of hours that drivers can operate a commercial vehicle, and rest requirements for drivers.

- Environmental regulations: Environmental regulations set standards for the emission of pollutants from commercial vehicles, and require transportation businesses to take steps to reduce their impact on the environment.

In conclusion, navigating the legal and regulatory requirements of your transportation business can be complex and time-consuming. By understanding the laws and regulations that apply, obtaining the required licenses and permits, complying with insurance requirements, and ensuring compliance with safety and environmental regulations, you'll be better equipped to start and operate your transportation business with confidence. In the next chapter, we'll discuss the importance of developing a strong business plan, and how to create a plan that meets your business goals and objectives.

Chapter 9. Financing Your Business: Securing Funding and Capital

Starting a transportation business can be expensive, and securing funding and capital is an important part of the process. In this chapter, we'll guide you through the process of financing your transportation business, and help you understand the different options available to you.

Determine Your Funding Needs

The first step in financing your transportation business is to determine your funding needs. This includes estimating the costs associated with starting and operating your business, including:

- Vehicle costs: The cost of purchasing or leasing vehicles for your transportation business.

- Equipment costs: The cost of purchasing equipment, such as trailers and cargo containers.

- Operating costs: The cost of operating your business, including fuel, insurance, maintenance, and more.

- Marketing costs: The cost of marketing and promoting your transportation business.

Understand Your Financing Options

Once you've determined your funding needs, the next step is to understand your financing options. Some of the most common financing options for transportation businesses include:

- Bank loans: Bank loans are a common form of financing for transportation businesses. To obtain a loan, you'll typically need to provide collateral, such as equipment or real estate, and have a strong credit history.

- SBA loans: The Small Business Administration (SBA) provides loan guarantees to small businesses, which can help you secure financing for your transportation business.

- Grants: Grants are a form of financing that does not need to be repaid. You can find grants for transportation businesses by searching for grants for small businesses, or by contacting your state or local government.

- Crowdfunding: Crowdfunding is a form of financing that allows you to raise funds from a large number of people, usually through the internet.

Develop a Strong Business Plan

No matter which financing option you choose, having a strong business plan is essential. A business plan is a document that outlines your business goals and objectives, and provides a roadmap for starting and operating your transportation business.

In your business plan, you'll want to include information about your:

- Market analysis: A description of the transportation industry and your competition.

- Service offerings: A description of the services you plan to offer.

- Marketing strategy: Your plan for attracting customers and building brand awareness.

- Financial projections: Your estimated costs and earnings.

- Operations and logistics: Your plan for executing your services.

Having a strong business plan will make it easier to secure financing and capital, and help you attract investors and lenders who believe in your vision for your transportation business.

In conclusion, financing your transportation business is an important part of starting and operating a successful business. By determining your funding needs, understanding your financing options, and developing a strong business plan, you'll be better equipped to secure the funding and capital you need to succeed. In the next chapter, we'll discuss the importance of developing a marketing strategy, and how to create a strategy that attracts customers and builds brand awareness.

Chapter 10. Human Resources: Building a Strong Team

One of the most important aspects of starting and operating a successful transportation business is building a strong team of employees. A talented and dedicated team can help you provide excellent services to your customers, and drive your business forward. In this chapter, we'll guide you through the process of building a strong team, and help you understand the key considerations you'll need to make along the way.

Determine Your Staffing Needs

The first step in building a strong team is to determine your staffing needs. This includes estimating the number of employees you'll need, and identifying the roles and responsibilities you'll need to fill. Some common roles in a transportation business include:

- Drivers: The employees who operate your vehicles and transport goods.

- Dispatchers: The employees who manage the scheduling and routing of your vehicles.

- Mechanics: The employees who maintain and repair your vehicles.

- Customer service: The employees who interact with your customers and provide support.

Develop a Hiring Plan

Once you've determined your staffing needs, the next step is to develop a hiring plan. This includes creating job descriptions for each role, and outlining your hiring process. Some key elements of a hiring plan include:

- Job descriptions: Detailed descriptions of the roles you'll be hiring for, including the responsibilities, qualifications, and desired experience.

- Recruitment process: Your plan for finding and attracting candidates, including job postings, networking, and employee referrals.

- Interview process: Your plan for conducting interviews, including the questions you'll ask, and the criteria you'll use to evaluate candidates.

Hire the Right People

One of the most important parts of building a strong team is hiring the right people. You want to find employees who are:

- Skilled and knowledgeable: You want employees who are knowledgeable and experienced in their field, and who have the skills to perform their duties.

- Customer-focused: You want employees who are committed to providing excellent customer service, and who are always striving to meet and exceed customer expectations.

- Dedicated and reliable: You want employees who are committed to their work, and who are always willing to go above and beyond to get the job done.

Invest in Employee Development

Another key aspect of building a strong team is investing in employee development. This includes providing opportunities for employees to grow and advance in their careers, and investing in their training and development. Some ways to invest in employee development include:

- On-the-job training: Providing employees with opportunities to learn and develop new skills while they're working.

- Professional development programs: Offering employees opportunities to attend workshops, seminars, and conferences, or to take online courses.

- Leadership development: Investing in the development of your employees as leaders, so they can take on more responsibility and advance in their careers.

Provide a Positive Work Environment

Finally, it's important to create a positive work environment for your employees. This includes:

- Providing competitive compensation and benefits: Offering competitive pay and benefits, such as health insurance and paid time off, to attract and retain talented employees.

- Encouraging work-life balance: Providing flexible work arrangements, such as flexible schedules and telecommuting options, to help employees balance their work and personal lives.

- Recognizing and rewarding employees: Providing opportunities for employees to be recognized and rewarded for their hard work and achievements.

Chapter 11. Technology: Enhancing Efficiency and Customer Experience

Technology has become an essential part of every business, including the transportation industry. The use of technology can help to streamline operations, increase efficiency, and improve the overall customer experience. In this chapter, we will explore how you can use technology to your advantage when starting and running your transportation business.

First and foremost, you will need to assess what technology you will need to effectively run your business. This may include software for scheduling and dispatch, GPS tracking and monitoring, and digital payment methods. You will also need to consider the cost of these tools and how they fit into your overall budget.

In addition to these essential tools, there are other ways that you can use technology to stand out from the competition. This may include offering mobile applications for booking services, providing real-time updates to customers, and incorporating cutting-edge safety features such as in-vehicle cameras and tracking devices.

Finally, it's important to remember that technology is constantly evolving, so it's important to stay up-to-date on the latest advancements and trends. By being proactive and incorporating technology into your business plan, you can set your transportation company apart and provide a memorable and convenient experience for your customers.

In conclusion, technology is a crucial aspect of the transportation industry and should be carefully considered as part of your business plan. By using technology to your advantage, you can streamline operations, increase efficiency, and improve the overall customer experience, helping you to achieve long-term success.

Chapter 12.   Cost-Saving Strategies: Minimizing Operating Costs

Starting and running a transportation business can be costly, but there are ways to minimize operating costs and maximize profits. In this chapter, we will discuss some cost-saving strategies that you can implement to help keep your business financially healthy.

One of the most important cost-saving strategies is to carefully manage your expenses. This may include tracking your spending, negotiating better deals with suppliers, and reducing waste wherever possible. You should also look for opportunities to save money on fuel, maintenance, and insurance costs.

Another important strategy is to optimize your routes and schedules. By finding the most efficient and cost-effective ways to transport goods and people, you can reduce operating costs and improve your bottom line. This may involve using GPS and route planning software, as well as regularly reviewing your routes and making adjustments as needed.

In addition, it's important to invest in quality equipment and vehicles that are reliable and cost-effective to maintain. This can help to minimize downtime and reduce maintenance costs, as well as improve the overall customer experience.

Finally, consider partnering with other transportation businesses to share resources and reduce costs. This may include pooling resources for maintenance and repairs, or working together on joint marketing campaigns to reach a wider audience.

In conclusion, there are many strategies you can implement to minimize operating costs and keep your transportation business financially healthy. By carefully managing your expenses, optimizing your routes and schedules, investing in quality equipment, and partnering with other businesses, you can increase your profits and achieve long-term success.

Chapter 13. Strategic Planning: Mapping Out Your Path to Success

Starting a transportation business is a big step, but with careful planning, you can set yourself up for success. In this chapter, we will discuss the importance of strategic planning and provide tips for mapping out your path to success.

Strategic planning is the process of setting goals and developing a plan to achieve those goals. This includes identifying your target market, analyzing your competition, and determining what sets your business apart. It's also important to identify potential risks and challenges, and develop a plan to mitigate them.

One of the most important steps in strategic planning is to determine your target market. Who will your customers be, and what are their needs and preferences? Knowing your target market will help you to develop a marketing strategy that will effectively reach them, and also inform your service offerings and pricing structure.

Once you have determined your target market, it's important to analyze your competition. What are your competitors offering, and how can you differentiate yourself from them? You should also consider the size and growth potential of the market, and whether there is enough demand to support your business.

Another important aspect of strategic planning is to determine your business's unique selling proposition (USP). This is what sets your business apart from the competition and makes it unique. Your USP may be based on the quality of your services, the level of customer service you provide, or the technology you use.

Finally, it's important to set achievable and realistic goals for your business, and develop a plan to achieve those goals. This may involve setting specific targets for revenue, growth, and customer acquisition, and regularly tracking your progress towards these goals.

In conclusion, strategic planning is an essential part of starting and running a successful transportation business. By carefully analyzing your target market, competition, and unique selling proposition, and setting achievable goals, you can map out your path to success and achieve long-term growth and prosperity.

Chapter 14. Customer Service: Providing Exceptional Service to Your Clients

When it comes to running a successful transportation business, providing excellent customer service is key. In this chapter, we will discuss the importance of customer service, and provide tips for delivering exceptional service to your clients.

Customer service is all about meeting the needs and expectations of your customers. It's about creating a positive experience for them, and leaving them with a lasting impression of your business. A strong focus on customer service can help you to build a loyal customer base, and encourage positive word-of-mouth referrals.

One of the key components of great customer service is effective communication. You should make sure that you respond promptly to customer inquiries, and that you provide clear and concise information. This includes ensuring that your customers are well informed about your services, and that they understand any policies or procedures related to your business.

Another important aspect of customer service is reliability. You should make sure that your services are delivered on time, and that any problems or issues are resolved promptly. This includes having a contingency plan in place in case of unexpected disruptions or delays.

In addition to reliability, it's important to provide a high level of quality in your services. This means ensuring that your vehicles are well-maintained and in good condition, and that your drivers are knowledgeable and professional. It's also important to provide a safe and comfortable ride for your customers.

Another key element of great customer service is providing value for money. You should make sure that your prices are competitive, and that you provide a good value for the services that you offer. You can also provide additional services, such as in-car entertainment, to help enhance the customer experience.

Finally, it's important to show appreciation for your customers. This may include sending thank-you notes, offering loyalty programs, or providing special discounts and promotions. These gestures help to build a strong relationship with your customers, and encourage them to continue using your services.

In conclusion, customer service is a crucial part of running a successful transportation business. By focusing on effective communication, reliability, quality, value for money, and appreciation, you can provide exceptional service to your clients and build a loyal customer base.

Chapter 15. Sales and Business Development: Growing Your Business

Now that you have a solid foundation for your transportation business, it's time to start thinking about growth. In this chapter, we will discuss strategies for sales and business development, and provide tips for expanding your business and reaching new customers.

One of the most important things you can do for your business is to develop a solid sales plan. This should include a clear definition of your target market, as well as a strategy for reaching those customers. This may include tactics such as direct mail, online advertising, and cold calling.

Another important aspect of sales and business development is networking. This means connecting with other businesses and individuals in your industry, as well as in your local community. Networking can help you to build relationships, and can provide opportunities for joint ventures, partnerships, and cross-promotions.

In addition to networking, it's important to focus on building your brand. This includes creating a strong, memorable logo and tagline, as well as developing a consistent look and feel for all of your marketing materials. You should also focus on creating a strong online presence, which includes a professional website, social media accounts, and search engine optimization.

Another key component of business development is expanding your services. This may include adding new transportation options, such as luxury vehicles or limousines, or offering new services, such as airport transfers or corporate events. You should also consider expanding into new geographic markets, such as other cities or countries.

To support your business growth, it's important to have a strong team in place. This includes hiring skilled sales and marketing professionals, as well as investing in training and development for your employees. You should also focus on building a positive company culture, which can help to attract and retain top talent.

Finally, it's important to be flexible and open-minded. The transportation industry is constantly evolving, and you need to be willing to adapt and change with it. This means being open to new ideas and technologies, and being willing to experiment with new strategies and techniques.

In conclusion, sales and business development are critical components of growing your transportation business. By developing a solid sales plan, networking, building your brand, expanding your services, investing in your team, and being flexible, you can increase your customer base and achieve long-term success.

Chapter 16. Industry Trends: Staying Ahead of the Competition

As the transportation industry continues to grow and evolve, it's important to stay up-to-date on the latest trends and developments. In this chapter, we will discuss the current state of the industry, and provide tips for staying ahead of the competition.

One of the most important trends in the transportation industry is the increasing demand for eco-friendly and sustainable solutions. This includes the use of hybrid and electric vehicles, as well as alternative fuel sources such as natural gas and biofuels. As a result, it's important for transportation businesses to consider incorporating these options into their fleets, as well as promoting their commitment to sustainability in their marketing materials.

Another trend in the industry is the growing use of technology, particularly in the area of ride-hailing services. Companies like Uber and Lyft have disrupted the traditional taxi and limousine businesses, and have set a new standard for convenience and ease of use. To stay competitive, it's important for transportation businesses to invest in technology and offer similar services to their customers.

In addition to technology, there is a growing trend towards personalization and customization in the transportation industry. Customers want more than just a ride from point A to point B – they want a unique, personalized experience. This may include custom music playlists, in-car entertainment, and personalized concierge services. By offering these types of services, transportation businesses can differentiate themselves from the competition and provide a higher level of customer satisfaction.

Another trend in the industry is the use of data and analytics. Companies are using data to track and analyze their operations, as well as to make informed decisions about pricing, marketing, and other business initiatives. To stay competitive, it's important for transportation businesses to invest in data and analytics, and use this information to drive business growth and improve customer experience.

Finally, there is a growing trend towards collaboration and partnerships in the transportation industry. Companies are working together to offer bundled services, joint marketing initiatives, and cross-promotions. By collaborating with other businesses, transportation companies can reach new customers, increase brand awareness, and improve their overall competitiveness.

In conclusion, staying ahead of the competition in the transportation industry requires an understanding of current trends and a willingness to adapt and evolve. By focusing on sustainability, technology, personalization, data and analytics, and collaboration, transportation businesses can stay ahead of the curve and achieve long-term success.

Chapter 17. Safety and Security: Ensuring Safe Operations

As a transportation business, ensuring the safety and security of your customers, employees, and equipment is of the utmost importance. Not only is it a moral obligation, but it is also a legal requirement to maintain the highest standards of safety and security. In this chapter, we'll explore the various measures that you can take to guarantee a safe and secure operation.

First and foremost, it's essential to understand the regulations and laws that govern the transportation industry. Depending on the type of services you provide, there may be specific rules and guidelines that you must follow. For example, if you're operating a commercial trucking company, you'll need to adhere to the Federal Motor Carrier Safety Administration's regulations. Similarly, if you provide air transportation, you'll be subject to the Federal Aviation Administration's regulations. Familiarizing yourself with the applicable laws and regulations is a critical step in ensuring a safe and secure operation.

One of the most critical aspects of safety and security is maintaining your vehicles and equipment. This includes regular maintenance and inspections to ensure that your vehicles are in top condition, as well as implementing preventative measures to reduce the risk of accidents and malfunctions. For example, you may choose to install GPS tracking systems, backup cameras, and automatic braking systems to help improve the safety of your vehicles.

Another essential component of safety and security is the training and education of your employees. This includes providing proper training for drivers and technicians, as well as educating employees on the importance of following safety protocols and procedures. It's also crucial to have emergency response plans in place and to conduct regular drills to ensure that everyone knows what to do in the event of an emergency.

Finally, it's crucial to have proper insurance coverage in place. This includes liability insurance to protect you and your business in the event of an accident, as well as insurance to cover the cost of repairs or replacement of your vehicles and equipment.

In conclusion, maintaining the highest standards of safety and security is not only the right thing to do, but it's also critical to the success of your transportation business. By understanding the laws and regulations, maintaining your vehicles and equipment, training your employees, and having proper insurance coverage in place, you'll be well on your way to providing a safe and secure operation for your customers and employees.

Chapter 18. Environmental Sustainability: Implementing Green Practices

As a business in the transportation industry, it's important to not only focus on profit and success, but also to consider the impact your business has on the environment. With increasing awareness about climate change and the importance of sustainability, it's important to incorporate green practices into your business plan.

Here are some ways you can implement environmental sustainability into your transportation business:

1. Fuel Efficiency: Consider investing in vehicles that run on alternative fuels, such as electric or hybrid vehicles, which will not only save on operating costs but also reduce your carbon footprint.

2. Energy Efficiency: Reduce energy waste by installing energy-efficient lighting and heating/cooling systems in your offices, vehicles, and storage facilities.

3. Waste Management: Implement a waste management program that focuses on reducing, reusing, and recycling. This can include separating recyclables, composting, and reducing paper waste.

4. Green Logistics: Optimize your delivery routes to reduce fuel consumption and emissions. This includes considering the most efficient routes, grouping deliveries, and utilizing technology such as GPS to track and optimize routes.

5. Carbon Footprint: Consider offsetting your carbon footprint by investing in carbon credits or supporting environmental initiatives.

By incorporating these green practices into your business plan, you not only show your commitment to the environment, but you can also attract environmentally-conscious customers who are willing to pay a premium for eco-friendly services.

So, as you create your transportation business plan, be sure to include a section on environmental sustainability and the measures you'll take to minimize your impact on the planet. It's a small step, but it's one that can make a big difference in the long run.

Chapter 19. Insurance and Risk Management: Protecting Your Business

Running a transportation business can come with a lot of risks and uncertainties, from accidents and liability to theft and natural disasters. That's why it's important to have a strong risk management plan in place to protect your business and ensure its continued success.

Here are some important areas to consider when it comes to insurance and risk management for your transportation business:

1. Liability Insurance: This type of insurance covers you in the event of accidents or incidents involving your vehicles, employees, or customers. This includes coverage for personal injury, property damage, and medical expenses.

2. Vehicle Insurance: Protect your vehicles with insurance that covers theft, collision, and other types of damage. You may also want to consider additional coverage such as road side assistance or rental car reimbursement.

3. Business Interruption Insurance: This type of insurance can provide financial assistance in the event of a disruption to your operations, such as a natural disaster or power outage.

4. Workers' Compensation: This insurance is required by law in most states and covers the medical expenses of employees who are injured on the job.

5. Cyber Liability Insurance: In today's digital age, it's important to protect your business against cyber attacks and data breaches. This type of insurance can help cover the costs of responding to an attack and restoring your business operations.

In addition to insurance, it's also important to implement effective risk management strategies to minimize potential threats to your business. This can include conducting regular safety inspections, implementing security protocols, and training employees on how to handle emergency situations.

So, as you create your transportation business plan, be sure to include a section on insurance and risk management. Having the right insurance coverage and risk management strategies in place can provide peace of mind and help protect your business from unexpected setbacks.

Chapter 20. Contract Negotiations: Securing Fair Agreements

When starting a transportation business, one of the most important aspects to consider is the contracts that you will be entering into with clients and suppliers. These agreements can have a significant impact on your bottom line, so it is important to ensure that they are fair and equitable for both parties.

One of the key steps in contract negotiations is identifying what you need from the agreement. This might include things like delivery dates, payment terms, and any specific requirements for the services you will be providing. Once you have a clear understanding of what you need, you can begin negotiating with the other party.

When negotiating a contract, it is important to be transparent about your intentions and expectations. You should be willing to listen to the other party's concerns and work together to find a mutually acceptable solution. In many cases, a little give and take is necessary in order to reach a fair agreement.

Another key consideration when negotiating contracts is to make sure that you have the right protections in place. This might include things like liability insurance, performance bonds, and dispute resolution mechanisms. By including these elements in your contracts, you can reduce your risk and protect your business from potential legal or financial problems.

Finally, it is important to remember that contracts are not set in stone. You can always revisit them and make changes if necessary. For example, if you need to adjust the delivery schedule for a project, you can work with the other party to renegotiate the terms of the contract.

By taking the time to carefully negotiate contracts and secure fair agreements, you can protect your business and ensure its long-term success.

Chapter 21. International Trade: Expanding Your Business Globally

Expanding your transportation business to the global market can be both exciting and challenging. The world of international trade can be complex, but with careful planning and preparation, your business can successfully navigate the process. In this chapter, we'll explore the opportunities and challenges of international trade and what you need to consider when taking your business global.

Understanding the Global Market

Before diving into international trade, it's important to understand the market you're entering. Researching the demand for your services in different countries and understanding the local business culture can help you make informed decisions about expanding your business. Some factors to consider include:

- Market demand: Is there a need for your services in the country you're considering expanding to? What are the current market conditions and how do they impact the demand for your services?

- Business culture: Each country has its own business culture, with different customs and practices. Understanding these cultural differences can help you tailor your approach and make more effective business decisions.

- Regulations and compliance: Each country has its own laws and regulations, including those related to transportation. Ensure that you understand the regulations and requirements for operating in the country you're considering expanding to.

Developing a Global Business Plan

Once you have a clear understanding of the market, it's time to start developing a business plan. Your plan should consider the following:

- Logistics: Shipping and customs processes can be complex, so you need to ensure that you have a clear understanding of how your goods will be transported to the target market.

- Marketing: How will you reach your target market and build brand awareness? Developing a marketing plan that considers cultural differences and local market conditions is key to success.

- Financing: Expanding your business globally can be expensive, so it's important to secure the necessary financing to ensure success.

- Legal and regulatory requirements: Ensure that you understand the legal and regulatory requirements for operating in the country you're expanding to. This may include obtaining licenses and permits, as well as complying with tax laws and labor regulations.

Partnering with Local Companies

Partnering with local companies can be a great way to build relationships and gain a deeper understanding of the local market. This can also help you navigate the challenges of international trade and avoid potential pitfalls. When considering a local partner, consider the following:

- Reputation: Look for a partner with a strong reputation and a track record of success in the local market.

- Expertise: Ensure that your partner has the expertise and knowledge to help you succeed in the local market.

- Relationships: Building relationships with local companies and organizations can help you establish a strong network of support.

- Financial stability: Partnering with a financially stable company can help reduce the risks associated with international trade.

Expanding your transportation business globally can be a rewarding experience, but it requires careful planning and preparation. By understanding the market, developing a solid business plan, and partnering with local companies, you can successfully navigate the challenges of international trade and take your business to the next level.

Chapter 22. Logistics Planning: Ensuring Efficient Operations

Transportation and logistics are at the heart of your business, so it's crucial to get it right. Logistics planning is all about making sure that your operations run smoothly and efficiently. From choosing the right suppliers to finding the best routes and delivery methods, every detail is important. In this chapter, we'll take a closer look at what logistics planning entails and how to make sure it works for you.

First, let's define logistics. Logistics is the process of planning, implementing, and controlling the movement of goods from one place to another. It encompasses everything from procurement to delivery. Your logistics plan should outline the best way to move your goods from the point of origin to the final destination.

To create a solid logistics plan, you need to consider a few key factors. Firstly, you need to understand your customers' needs. What are their delivery expectations? How quickly do they need their products? Once you have a clear understanding of their needs, you can start to develop your logistics plan.

Next, consider the different modes of transportation available to you. Depending on your business, you may use air, sea, or ground transportation. Each mode has its own advantages and disadvantages, so it's important to choose the right one for your business. For example, air transportation is generally the fastest but also the most expensive, while sea transportation is slower but often more cost-effective.

Once you've chosen your mode of transportation, you need to think about the routes you'll use. This will depend on your customers' locations and the availability of transportation. You should also consider factors like transit time and the cost of shipping. You may need to explore different routes and shipping methods to find the best option for your business.

Finally, you need to make sure that your logistics plan is efficient. This means minimizing waste, reducing costs, and optimizing your operations. For example, you may need to invest in technology like GPS tracking and routing software to help you keep track of your deliveries and ensure they arrive on time.

In conclusion, logistics planning is crucial for the success of your transportation business. By understanding your customers' needs, choosing the right mode of transportation, developing efficient routes, and optimizing your operations, you'll be able to deliver products to your customers quickly and cost-effectively. Remember, the better your logistics plan, the more successful your business will be!

Chapter 23. Performance Metrics: Measuring Success and Making Adjustments

As a transportation business owner, it's crucial to understand the key performance metrics that will help you measure success and make informed decisions about the future of your company. In this chapter, we'll explore the various metrics you should be tracking and why they're important.

First and foremost, you should be monitoring your revenue. This will give you a clear picture of how much money you're bringing in and whether or not your business is profitable. You should also be tracking your expenses, including operating costs, marketing and advertising expenses, and any other costs associated with running your business. This will help you identify areas where you may be able to cut costs or reduce expenses.

Another important metric to track is customer satisfaction. You can measure this by conducting surveys, tracking customer reviews, or tracking repeat business. This will give you an idea of how happy your customers are with your services and whether or not they're likely to recommend your business to others.

In addition, you should be monitoring the efficiency of your operations. This includes tracking the speed and reliability of your deliveries, the number of accidents or incidents on the road, and the amount of time it takes to complete a job. All of these metrics can help you identify areas where you can improve and make changes that will help your business run more smoothly.

Finally, it's important to track your market share. This will give you an idea of how well you're competing against other transportation businesses in your area and will help you determine whether or not you need to make changes to your services or marketing strategy.

In conclusion, performance metrics are essential to the success of your transportation business. By tracking these metrics and making adjustments as necessary, you can ensure that your business is operating efficiently, providing high-quality services, and growing in the right direction.

Chapter 24. Leadership and Management: Leading Your Team to Success

As the owner or manager of a transportation business, you will be the driving force behind your company's success. Your leadership style, decision-making ability, and management skills will determine the course of your business and the outcome of your efforts.

Leadership

Leadership is about setting a vision, inspiring your team, and guiding your business towards success. It is essential to be able to communicate effectively, delegate responsibilities, and maintain a positive work environment. A great leader will have the ability to motivate their team and bring out their best efforts. You should have a clear understanding of your values, mission, and goals, and communicate them to your team.

Management

Management is the day-to-day operations of your business, including planning, organizing, and controlling the activities of your team. Effective management is key to ensuring that your business runs smoothly and meets its goals. A good manager will have strong problem-solving skills, decision-making ability, and an understanding of the needs of their team. They will also be able to communicate effectively and create a positive work environment.

Building a Strong Team

Having a strong team is crucial to the success of your transportation business. Your team members should be knowledgeable, skilled, and motivated. It is important to invest in your employees and provide them with the training and support they need to perform their jobs effectively. In turn, your employees will be more productive, engaged, and motivated to contribute to the success of your business.

Leadership and management are essential components of a successful transportation business. By developing your skills in these areas and building a strong team, you will be well-equipped to guide your business to success.

Chapter 25. Innovation and Entrepreneurship: Staying Ahead of the Curve

As a transportation business owner, it's essential to stay ahead of the curve and be innovative in order to stand out in the industry. The world of transportation is constantly changing and evolving, so being innovative and entrepreneurial is key to success. Here are a few tips to help you stay ahead of the game:

1. Stay up-to-date with industry trends: Keeping abreast of the latest industry trends is crucial for staying ahead of the competition. Read trade magazines, attend industry conferences and events, and stay connected with industry associations.

2. Utilize technology: Technology is revolutionizing the transportation industry, and it's essential to embrace it to stay ahead. From GPS systems to automated dispatch, there are many ways to incorporate technology into your operations.

3. Be flexible: The transportation industry is constantly changing, and being flexible allows you to adapt to these changes and stay ahead of the curve. Be open to trying new things, and be willing to pivot your business strategy if necessary.

4. Encourage innovation: Encourage your team to come up with new and innovative ideas. Encourage them to think outside the box and challenge the status quo.

5. Network: Networking with other transportation professionals is a great way to stay ahead of the curve. Attend industry events, join industry associations, and connect with other business owners and entrepreneurs.

Being innovative and entrepreneurial is essential for success in the transportation industry. By staying up-to-date with industry trends, utilizing technology, being flexible, encouraging innovation, and networking, you can stay ahead of the curve and succeed in this competitive industry.

Chapter 26. Financial Management: Keeping Your Business Financially Sound

As a transportation business owner, financial management is a crucial aspect of your success. This includes keeping track of expenses, generating revenue, and making informed financial decisions that ensure the stability and growth of your company. In this chapter, we'll explore the various aspects of financial management, and how you can use them to create a strong foundation for your transportation business.

Bookkeeping and Record Keeping

One of the most important aspects of financial management is keeping accurate records of your financial transactions. This includes keeping track of expenses, revenue, and other financial activities. By doing this, you can get a clear picture of your financial standing, and make informed decisions about where to allocate your resources.

You can keep track of your financial records manually, or you can use software tools such as QuickBooks, Xero, or MYOB. These tools can help you keep track of your expenses, generate reports, and make informed decisions about your financial future.

Budgeting and Forecasting

Another important aspect of financial management is budgeting and forecasting. This involves projecting your future expenses and revenue, and making informed decisions about how you can allocate your resources to achieve your business goals. This can help you avoid overspending, and make sure that you have enough funds available to meet your financial obligations.

To create a budget and forecast, you can use a spreadsheet or a software tool, and input your projected expenses and revenue. You can then compare your actual financial performance against your projections, and make any necessary adjustments to keep your finances on track.

Financial Statements

Financial statements are a key part of financial management. They provide a comprehensive overview of your financial standing, and include reports such as your income statement, balance sheet, and cash flow statement.

The income statement provides an overview of your revenue, expenses, and net profit or loss. The balance sheet provides an overview of your assets, liabilities, and equity. The cash flow statement provides a detailed overview of your cash inflows and outflows, and how they affect your overall financial health.

By reviewing your financial statements, you can get a better understanding of your financial standing, and make informed decisions about your business future.

Cost-Saving Strategies

Finally, it's important to implement cost-saving strategies to minimize your expenses and maximize your profit margins. This can include reducing your overhead costs, negotiating better deals with suppliers, and finding ways to reduce your operational costs.

For example, you can invest in energy-efficient technology, adopt green practices, or implement a telecommuting policy to reduce your office expenses. By reducing your costs, you can increase your profit margins, and secure the financial stability of your transportation business.

In conclusion, financial management is a critical aspect of your transportation business success. By keeping accurate records, budgeting and forecasting, reviewing your financial statements, and implementing cost-saving strategies, you can create a strong foundation for your business and achieve your financial goals.

Chapter 27. Marketing and Branding: Building Your Reputation and Growing Your Business

Building a strong brand and marketing strategy is essential to growing your transportation business. Your marketing strategy will help you reach new customers, retain existing customers, and build your business's reputation in the industry.

To create a successful marketing strategy, you'll need to do some research to understand your target audience. Who are your customers? What do they need and want from your transportation services? What motivates them to choose your business over your competitors? Answering these questions will help you develop a marketing plan that resonates with your target audience.

Once you have a clear understanding of your target audience, you can start developing your marketing strategy. Some effective marketing tactics for transportation businesses include:

- Creating a website that showcases your services and provides customers with easy-to-use booking and scheduling tools

- Utilizing social media platforms to reach new customers and engage with existing customers

- Implementing email marketing campaigns to keep customers informed about new services and promotions

- Developing partnerships with complementary businesses to reach new customers and increase brand awareness

In addition to your marketing tactics, you'll also want to develop a strong brand identity. This includes creating a logo, tagline, and color scheme that represents your business and sets you apart from your competitors. Your brand should be reflected in all of your marketing materials, from your website to your business cards.

Finally, don't forget to measure the success of your marketing efforts. Keep track of your website traffic, social media engagement, and conversion rates. Use this data to make adjustments to your marketing strategy and continue to grow your business.

Investing in your marketing and branding strategy will pay off in the long run, as you'll be able to reach new customers and establish a strong reputation in the transportation industry.

Chapter 28. Human Resources: Attracting and Retaining Top Talent

As a transportation business owner, you know that your team is the backbone of your operations. Without top talent, your business is unlikely to thrive. That's why it's important to prioritize your human resources strategy. In this chapter, we'll explore how to attract and retain the best people for your team.

Attracting Top Talent

Attracting top talent to your business is all about having a compelling offer. This includes things like a competitive salary, great benefits, opportunities for growth and development, and a supportive work environment. You can also differentiate yourself from the competition by offering unique perks or work arrangements, such as flexible hours or the ability to work from home.

When you're recruiting, be sure to focus on finding the right fit for your business. This means looking for people who share your values and mission, as well as those who have the skills and experience necessary to excel in the roles you're hiring for. It also means being open and honest about your expectations, so candidates know what they're getting into before they join your team.

Retaining Top Talent

Once you've attracted top talent, it's important to keep them engaged and motivated. This means providing opportunities for growth and development, offering fair compensation and benefits, and fostering a positive work environment.

Another key factor in retaining top talent is communication. Regular check-ins and performance reviews give employees the opportunity to provide feedback and hear how they're doing. This not only helps you identify areas for improvement, but it also lets your employees know that you're invested in their success.

Leadership and management play a critical role in retaining top talent. This means setting clear expectations and providing the resources and support employees need to do their best work. It also means recognizing and rewarding their contributions, so they feel valued and appreciated.

Final Thoughts

Attracting and retaining top talent is essential to the success of your transportation business. By offering a compelling offer, focusing on the right fit, and supporting your team with regular communication, opportunities for growth, and leadership and management, you'll be well on your way to building a strong, motivated team that will drive your business to new heights.

Chapter 29. Employee Relations: Building Strong Relationships with Your Team

As a transportation business owner, it's important to remember that your employees are your biggest asset. Without them, your business wouldn't be able to operate, let alone succeed. That's why building strong relationships with your team is essential to the success of your business.

Employee relations can encompass a variety of aspects of your business, including employee engagement, communication, and feedback. Let's take a closer look at each of these areas.

Employee Engagement

Employee engagement refers to the level of involvement and enthusiasm that your employees have for their work. When employees are engaged, they're more likely to be productive, motivated, and committed to the success of your business.

One way to increase employee engagement is to clearly communicate your company's mission, values, and goals. When employees understand why they're doing what they're doing, they're more likely to feel a sense of purpose and be motivated to do their best work.

Communication

Clear and effective communication is key to building strong relationships with your employees. It's important to communicate regularly with your team, sharing updates and news about the business and asking for their thoughts and feedback. You should also encourage open and honest communication, allowing employees to share their thoughts and ideas without fear of retribution.

Feedback

Providing feedback to your employees is an important part of building strong relationships with them. Feedback can be both positive and negative, but it's important to always be constructive and respectful. Providing regular feedback can help employees understand their strengths and weaknesses, and it can help them improve their skills and performance.

In conclusion, building strong relationships with your employees is essential to the success of your transportation business. By focusing on employee engagement, communication, and feedback, you'll be able to create a positive work environment that fosters collaboration, creativity, and productivity.

Chapter 30. Legal Issues: Understanding and Navigating Legal Obligations

When starting or running a transportation business, it's important to understand the legal requirements and obligations that come along with it. Whether you're providing transportation services for people or goods, there are a variety of regulations and rules you need to be aware of to ensure your business operates smoothly and within the bounds of the law.

In this chapter, we'll go over some of the most important legal considerations to keep in mind when running a transportation business. By doing so, you'll be able to navigate the often complex world of business law and keep your operation running smoothly.

1.   Business Licenses and Permits

Before you start your transportation business, you'll need to obtain the necessary licenses and permits. This may include a business license, a commercial driver's license (CDL) for drivers, and a permit to operate vehicles in your state. It's important to research the specific requirements for your area and make sure you have all the necessary licenses and permits in place before you start your business.

2.   Insurance Requirements

Another important legal consideration is insurance. All transportation businesses must have liability insurance to protect against claims from third parties. This includes coverage for personal injury and property damage, as well as other liabilities that may arise from the operation of your business. It's also a good idea to have insurance for your vehicles and other assets, such as cargo, to ensure you're fully protected in the event of an accident or other loss.

3. Safety Regulations

Safety regulations play a big role in the transportation industry, and it's important to understand and follow all the rules and regulations that apply to your business. This includes everything from vehicle maintenance and inspection requirements to training and certification for drivers. Make sure you're aware of all the safety requirements and regulations that apply to your business and that you're in compliance with them at all times.

4. Contract Law

When you're working with clients or customers, you'll likely enter into contracts that outline the terms and conditions of your relationship. It's important to understand contract law and to have a clear and comprehensive agreement in place that protects your interests and sets expectations for both parties. This includes things like payment terms, delivery schedules, and any specific requirements or obligations you have as a service provider.

5. Labor Law

As an employer, it's also important to understand labor laws and to ensure you're in compliance with all the regulations that apply to your business. This includes everything from minimum wage requirements to overtime pay and benefits. Make sure you're aware of the labor laws that apply to your business and that you're treating your employees fairly and in accordance with the law.

In conclusion, the legal side of running a transportation business can seem overwhelming at times, but by understanding the key requirements and obligations, you can ensure your business operates smoothly and within the bounds of the law. By doing so, you'll be able to focus on growing and expanding your business, confident that you're doing so on a solid legal foundation.

Chapter 31. Operations and Maintenance: Maintaining Your Fleet and Operations

When it comes to operating a successful transportation business, keeping your fleet and operations in top shape is crucial. This involves a mix of proactive planning and reactive response to ensure that your vehicles and equipment are always ready to go. In this chapter, we will discuss how to develop an operations and maintenance plan that will keep your business running smoothly.

Start with a Preventive Maintenance Plan

Preventive maintenance is all about keeping your fleet and equipment in good condition before problems arise. This involves scheduling regular inspections and maintenance, such as oil changes, tire rotations, and brake checks, to keep your vehicles running at their best. By doing this, you can avoid costly breakdowns and repairs and extend the life of your equipment.

Implement an Effective Fleet Management System

To keep your operations running smoothly, it's important to have an effective fleet management system in place. This can include things like GPS tracking, vehicle maintenance records, and a driver behavior monitoring system. These tools will help you keep tabs on your vehicles and drivers, ensuring that they are all operating safely and efficiently.

Develop an Emergency Response Plan

No matter how well you plan and maintain your equipment, breakdowns and accidents can still happen. To be prepared, it's important to have an emergency response plan in place. This should include a clear understanding of who is responsible for what, what resources are available, and what steps should be taken to resolve the situation.

Stay Up-to-Date on Safety and Regulatory Requirements

In addition to maintaining your equipment, it's also important to stay up-to-date on safety and regulatory requirements. This includes things like proper licensing and certifications, compliance with safety standards, and following industry best practices. By staying up-to-date, you can ensure that your business is operating legally and safely, and you can avoid costly fines and penalties.

Invest in Employee Training

Your employees play a crucial role in the success of your operations and maintenance plan. To make sure they are equipped to handle any situation that arises, it's important to invest in employee training. This can include things like vehicle maintenance training, emergency response training, and driver safety training. By providing your employees with the tools and knowledge they need to succeed, you can ensure that your business runs smoothly and efficiently.

In conclusion, a well-planned operations and maintenance plan is essential for any transportation business. By taking the time to plan and prepare, you can ensure that your fleet and operations are always in top shape and ready to take on any challenge that comes your way. Whether you're just starting out or you've been in business for years, it's never too late to develop an effective plan that will keep your business running smoothly.

Chapter 32. Route Optimization: Streamlining Operations for Increased Efficiency

As a transportation business, one of the most important things you can do to increase efficiency and save time and money is to optimize your routes. Route optimization refers to the process of finding the most efficient route for your vehicles to travel, taking into account things like traffic, road conditions, distance, and time.

The first step in optimizing your routes is to identify the areas that need improvement. Take a close look at your current routes and consider what could be done differently to make them more efficient. Maybe there are areas where your vehicles are taking longer than they should, or areas where you could save time and fuel by taking a different route.

Once you have identified areas for improvement, it's time to start exploring your options. There are many tools and resources available that can help you optimize your routes, including GPS tracking systems, mapping software, and traffic and weather apps. These tools can help you plan routes that are more efficient and avoid areas that are likely to cause delays.

Another important consideration when optimizing your routes is to take into account the needs of your customers. Make sure you understand their needs and expectations, and plan routes that are convenient and efficient for them. Consider things like pickup and delivery times, and the time it takes to load and unload your vehicles.

In addition to using technology to optimize your routes, it's also important to make sure your team is well-trained and equipped to carry out their duties. Make sure they have the necessary skills, knowledge, and equipment to do their jobs effectively and efficiently. Regular training sessions can help keep your team up-to-date on best practices and help them stay informed about new tools and techniques for optimizing routes.

Finally, it's important to track and monitor your progress as you optimize your routes. Keep a close eye on key performance indicators like delivery times, fuel efficiency, and customer satisfaction, and make adjustments as needed to ensure you're meeting your goals and making the most of your resources.

In conclusion, route optimization is a crucial component of running a successful transportation business. By taking the time to identify areas for improvement, exploring your options, and tracking your progress, you can streamline your operations and increase efficiency, saving time and money in the process.

Chapter 33. Fleet Management: Optimizing Your Fleet Operations

As a transportation business owner, one of your most valuable assets is your fleet. Whether you have a few vehicles or a large fleet of trucks and trailers, it's important to manage your fleet effectively to maximize its efficiency, reduce costs, and ensure customer satisfaction. Fleet management is all about making the most of your resources and maximizing their value to your business. In this chapter, we'll explore some of the key elements of fleet management and how you can optimize your operations.

First, let's take a closer look at what fleet management entails. Fleet management is the process of planning, organizing, and overseeing all aspects of a transportation fleet. This includes everything from purchasing and maintaining vehicles, to managing drivers, to tracking fuel usage and expenses. Effective fleet management is critical to the success of any transportation business, as it helps you to:

- Reduce costs: By closely monitoring expenses and making changes to your operations, you can reduce costs and improve your bottom line.

- Improve customer satisfaction: A well-run fleet means you can provide timely and reliable service to your customers, which will help you to build a strong reputation and attract new business.

- Maintain compliance: With regulations constantly changing, it's important to stay up-to-date on the latest requirements and ensure that your fleet is compliant.

So, what are some of the key elements of fleet management? Here are a few to consider:

- Vehicle procurement and maintenance: This includes purchasing and maintaining vehicles, as well as determining the best time to replace them.

- Driver management: This includes hiring, training, and managing drivers, as well as tracking their performance and compliance with regulations.

- Fuel management: This involves tracking fuel usage and costs, and implementing strategies to reduce fuel consumption and expenses.

- Route optimization: This involves determining the most efficient routes for your vehicles, which can help to reduce fuel consumption and improve delivery times.

- Fleet tracking and monitoring: This includes tracking the location and performance of your vehicles in real-time, and using this information to make informed decisions about your operations.

So, how can you optimize your fleet operations? Here are a few tips to get you started:

- Invest in technology: Technology can help you to streamline your operations, reduce costs, and improve customer satisfaction. For example, GPS tracking systems can help you to monitor your vehicles in real-time, while fleet management software can help you to manage all aspects of your fleet from one central location.

- Encourage driver safety: A safe and responsible driver is critical to the success of your business. Encourage your drivers to follow safe driving practices and provide them with the tools and training they need to succeed.

- Monitor fuel usage: Closely monitoring fuel usage and expenses can help you to identify areas for improvement and reduce costs. Consider implementing fuel-saving strategies, such as reducing idling time and optimizing routes.

- Communicate with your drivers: Regular communication with your drivers can help to build strong relationships and ensure that everyone is on the same page. Encourage your drivers to share feedback and suggestions, and take their input into consideration when making decisions about your operations.

In conclusion, fleet management is a critical component of any transportation business. By taking the time to plan, organize, and manage your fleet, you can optimize your operations, reduce costs, and improve customer satisfaction. Whether you're just starting out or have been in business for years, effective fleet management is essential for success. So take some time to evaluate your operations, identify areas for improvement, and implement the changes you need to grow and thrive.

Chapter 34. Technology and Automation: Enhancing Your Business with Cutting-Edge Solutions

As a transportation business, it's essential to keep up with the latest advancements in technology and automation. With the fast-paced advancements happening in the industry, you need to be able to adapt and leverage technology to keep up with the competition and improve the efficiency of your operations.

Investing in the right technology and automation tools can help you streamline your operations, reduce costs, and enhance the customer experience. From GPS tracking and real-time dispatching to automated invoicing and payment systems, there are numerous technology solutions that can help your business succeed.

Here are a few ways technology and automation can benefit your transportation business:

1. Improved efficiency: Automation helps eliminate manual processes, reducing errors and speeding up operations. This helps you to focus on other important tasks and reduce the workload of your employees.

2. Real-time tracking: With GPS tracking and real-time dispatching, you can monitor your vehicles and drivers in real-time. This helps you to track your fleet, ensure on-time delivery, and improve communication with customers.

3. Enhanced customer experience: Technology can help you offer a seamless experience for your customers. From mobile apps for booking and tracking services, to automated invoicing and payment systems, you can provide a convenient and hassle-free experience for your customers.

4. Increased safety: By leveraging technology, you can improve the safety of your operations. For example, you can use GPS tracking to monitor your vehicles and drivers, helping you to ensure they are operating safely and within the law.

When choosing the right technology and automation solutions for your business, it's important to assess your specific needs and goals. You may also want to consider factors such as the cost, ease of use, and level of integration with other systems and processes.

With the right technology and automation solutions in place, you can take your transportation business to the next level. By streamlining operations, reducing costs, and improving the customer experience, you can enhance the success of your business and stay ahead of the competition.

Chapter 35. Supply Chain Management: Streamlining Your Supply Chain Operations

As a transportation business, your supply chain plays a crucial role in ensuring the smooth delivery of goods and services to your customers. From sourcing materials and products to delivering them to their final destination, your supply chain has a direct impact on your business's efficiency and customer satisfaction.

That's why it's so important to optimize your supply chain operations. In this chapter, we'll explore the basics of supply chain management and some strategies for streamlining your operations for maximum efficiency and profitability.

The Basics of Supply Chain Management

Supply chain management is the process of overseeing and coordinating all the activities involved in getting a product from the manufacturer to the customer. This includes sourcing materials and products, production, transportation, warehousing, and delivery.

A well-managed supply chain can help your transportation business save time and money, while improving customer satisfaction and loyalty. On the other hand, a poorly managed supply chain can result in delays, increased costs, and dissatisfied customers.

Strategies for Streamlining Your Supply Chain Operations

1. Improve Visibility and Collaboration

One of the keys to a successful supply chain is having visibility into all aspects of the process. This includes knowing where your products are, when they will arrive, and what their condition is.

To achieve this, it's important to work closely with your suppliers and other stakeholders to ensure everyone is on the same page. This could include regular meetings and communication, as well as implementing tools like software or technology that allows for real-time tracking and collaboration.

2. Optimize Inventory Management

Inventory management is an important part of supply chain management, as it impacts both costs and customer satisfaction. By keeping your inventory levels optimized, you can reduce the cost of carrying inventory, minimize stock-outs, and improve your ability to fulfill orders quickly.

One way to optimize your inventory is to use just-in-time (JIT) inventory management. This involves only ordering what you need, when you need it, which can reduce the amount of inventory you need to carry and minimize the cost of storing and managing inventory.

3. Enhance Supply Chain Flexibility

A flexible supply chain can help you respond quickly to changes in demand, unexpected disruptions, and other challenges. This could include having multiple suppliers for key materials or products, implementing alternative transportation methods, or having backup plans in place for unanticipated events.

4. Implement Lean Supply Chain Management

Lean supply chain management is a strategy that emphasizes efficiency and waste reduction. This could involve reducing lead times, streamlining processes, and reducing inventory levels. By focusing on waste reduction, you can minimize costs, increase efficiency, and improve customer satisfaction.

5. Foster Strong Relationships with Suppliers

Your suppliers play a crucial role in the success of your supply chain. By fostering strong relationships with your suppliers, you can ensure that you have the materials and products you need when you need them, while also improving your ability to negotiate better terms and conditions.

6. Continuously Monitor and Improve

Finally, it's important to continuously monitor and improve your supply chain operations. This could involve regularly reviewing your processes, tracking key performance indicators (KPIs), and seeking feedback from customers and stakeholders. By continually looking for ways to improve your supply chain, you can stay ahead of the competition and deliver a better customer experience.

In conclusion, supply chain management is a critical part of your transportation business, and optimizing your operations can have a significant impact on your bottom line. By following the strategies outlined in this chapter, you can streamline your supply chain operations, reduce costs, and improve customer satisfaction.

Chapter 36. Emergency Planning and Response: Preparing for Unforeseeable Events

As a transportation business owner, it's important to plan for the unexpected. Emergencies can strike at any time and having a solid emergency response plan in place can help minimize the impact of these unforeseen events on your business. Whether it's a natural disaster, a sudden equipment failure, or a security breach, being prepared for any situation is key to ensuring the safety of your employees, customers, and assets.

So, what does a comprehensive emergency response plan entail? Here are some key elements to consider when putting together your plan:

1. Designate an emergency response team: Having a dedicated team in place to handle emergencies is crucial. This team should include representatives from different departments, including operations, human resources, and IT. This way, all aspects of the emergency can be addressed and managed effectively.

2. Assign roles and responsibilities: It's important to clearly define each team member's role in the event of an emergency. Who will be responsible for communicating with employees and customers? Who will be responsible for coordinating with outside agencies and emergency responders? Make sure everyone knows what they are

responsible for ahead of time so they can react quickly and effectively in an emergency situation.

3. Conduct regular drills and trainings: Regular drills and trainings can help your team become more familiar with the emergency response plan and build confidence in their ability to execute it. Make sure everyone understands what to do in different emergency scenarios and practice responding to those scenarios in a controlled environment.

4. Establish communication protocols: Communication is key in any emergency situation. Establish clear protocols for communicating with employees, customers, and outside agencies. Make sure everyone knows who to contact and how to reach them in case of an emergency.

5. Plan for different types of emergencies: Your emergency response plan should take into consideration different types of emergencies that could potentially impact your business, such as natural disasters, equipment failures, security breaches, and more. Plan for each scenario and make sure everyone is familiar with what to do in each situation.

6. Maintain and update the plan regularly: Your emergency response plan should be a living document that is regularly reviewed and updated to ensure it remains effective and relevant. Review the plan annually or after any significant changes to your operations or environment to make sure it stays up-to-date.

By taking the time to develop a comprehensive emergency response plan, you can give yourself and your team peace of mind knowing that you're prepared for anything that might come your way. With a plan in place, you'll be able to respond quickly and effectively to any emergency situation, minimizing the impact on your business and ensuring the safety of everyone involved.

Chapter 37. Customer Service: Providing Exceptional Customer Experience

At the heart of every successful transportation business is exceptional customer service. It's what sets your business apart from the competition and keeps your customers coming back. The key to providing a great customer experience is understanding what your customers need and want, and then delivering on those expectations.

The first step to delivering exceptional customer service is to develop a customer-centric culture within your business. This means that every member of your team, from the front-line employees to upper management, is committed to putting the customer first. You can do this by creating a customer service policy that sets expectations for all employees, as well as regular training programs that focus on customer service skills.

Another important aspect of delivering great customer service is having the right technology in place. This includes a robust customer relationship management (CRM) system, an easy-to-use website and booking system, and a mobile app that allows customers to easily track their shipments and communicate with you.

It's also important to have a system in place for handling customer complaints and resolving disputes. This can be a challenge, but with the right approach, you can turn even the most unhappy customers into lifelong advocates for your business. Start by listening to your customers' concerns, being empathetic, and offering solutions that meet their needs.

Another way to enhance your customer service is by being proactive. For example, you can send out regular newsletters or emails to keep your customers informed about your business and any special promotions or services you may be offering. You can also use social media platforms like Facebook and Twitter to engage with your customers and respond to their questions and comments.

Finally, it's essential to measure and track your customer service efforts. This can be done through regular customer surveys and feedback, as well as tracking metrics like customer satisfaction scores and customer retention rates. This information can then be used to make improvements and fine-tune your customer service approach.

In conclusion, providing exceptional customer service is essential to the success of your transportation business. By creating a customer-centric culture, investing in the right technology, handling customer complaints effectively, being proactive, and regularly measuring and tracking your efforts, you can deliver a truly memorable customer experience that sets your business apart from the competition.

Chapter 38. Network Expansion: Expanding Your Business Reach

As your transportation business grows, you may find yourself ready to expand your reach and reach new customers. Whether you're looking to expand your service area or move into new markets, there are a few key things to keep in mind. In this chapter, we'll explore the different strategies for expanding your business network and help you determine which approach is right for you.

1. Identifying Opportunities

The first step in expanding your business network is identifying opportunities for growth. This may mean exploring new markets or service areas, or finding new niches or customer segments to target. To identify opportunities, it's important to stay informed about the transportation industry, monitor trends and competitors, and gather information about customer needs and preferences.

2. Building Relationships

Building strong relationships with your customers is key to expanding your network. In order to build these relationships, you'll need to focus on providing high-quality service and developing a reputation for reliability and expertise. This can be accomplished through a variety of marketing strategies, including networking events, social media, and word of mouth marketing.

3. Developing a Marketing Plan

Once you've identified opportunities for growth and built relationships with your customers, it's time to develop a marketing plan. This plan should include strategies for reaching new customers, building your brand, and promoting your services. Some effective marketing strategies for expanding your network include online advertising, direct mail campaigns, and email marketing.

4. Investing in Technology

Investing in technology is another important factor in expanding your business network. For example, you may want to invest in transportation management software that helps you streamline your operations and keep track of your fleet and drivers. Additionally, you may want to invest in technologies that help you stay connected with your customers, such as GPS tracking and real-time updates.

5. Building a Strong Team

Finally, expanding your business network requires a strong and dedicated team. This means attracting and retaining top talent, and providing the support and resources your team needs to succeed. This can include providing ongoing training, offering competitive compensation and benefits, and creating a positive work environment.

Expanding your business network is a complex and ongoing process that requires careful planning and execution. However, with the right strategies and tools in place, you can grow your business and reach new customers, ultimately leading to increased success and profitability.

Chapter 39. Sustainability and Environmental Responsibility: Building a Greener Business

Introduction: In today's world, sustainability and environmental responsibility are increasingly important considerations for businesses of all sizes. Consumers are becoming more aware of the impact that companies have on the environment, and they are seeking out businesses that are making a positive difference. For transportation businesses, there are many opportunities to reduce your carbon footprint, minimize waste, and increase efficiency. By taking a proactive approach to sustainability and environmental responsibility, you can not only improve your reputation with customers, but also reduce your operating costs and increase profitability.

Why is Sustainability Important for Transportation Businesses? Transportation businesses have a significant impact on the environment. From the emissions generated by vehicles to the energy consumed by operations, transportation companies can contribute to a number of environmental problems. However, by taking a proactive approach to sustainability, transportation businesses can minimize their impact and become leaders in the industry.

Some benefits of building a greener business include:

- Improved reputation with customers and stakeholders
- Increased efficiency and reduced operating costs
- Compliance with environmental regulations
- Access to new business opportunities

How to Implement Sustainable Practices: There are many ways that transportation businesses can implement sustainable practices and become more environmentally responsible. Some of the most impactful strategies include:

1. Implementing energy-efficient technologies: By investing in energy-efficient technologies, such as electric vehicles, you can reduce your energy consumption and emissions.

2. Reducing waste: Implementing waste reduction strategies, such as recycling and composting programs, can help you minimize waste and reduce costs.

3. Improving fuel efficiency: By improving fuel efficiency, you can reduce emissions and save money on fuel costs.

4. Optimizing routes: By optimizing routes, you can reduce emissions and increase efficiency.

5. Encouraging alternative modes of transportation: Encouraging employees to use alternative modes of transportation, such as public transit or bicycles, can reduce emissions and promote a healthier lifestyle.

6. Partnering with suppliers and customers: By partnering with suppliers and customers who share your

commitment to sustainability, you can work together to minimize your impact on the environment.

7. Monitoring and reporting on sustainability efforts: By regularly monitoring and reporting on your sustainability efforts, you can demonstrate your commitment to the environment and make continuous improvements.

Conclusion: Building a greener business is an ongoing process that requires commitment and collaboration. By implementing sustainable practices and being proactive about environmental responsibility, transportation businesses can reduce their impact on the environment, improve their reputation, and increase profitability. Whether you are just starting out or looking to take your sustainability efforts to the next level, there are many opportunities to make a positive difference.

Chapter 40. Conclusion: Navigating the Transportation Industry with Confidence

So there you have it, folks! You've taken a journey through the many important components of a successful transportation business. From attracting and retaining top talent, to streamlining operations and enhancing customer experience, each piece plays a crucial role in your overall success.

As you navigate the industry, it's important to remember that no two businesses are exactly the same. There will always be unique challenges and opportunities that arise, but with a solid plan in place, you'll be ready to tackle anything that comes your way.

Take a moment to reflect on all that you've learned. Consider which areas may require some extra attention, and make sure to prioritize them. Keep in mind that your plan is a living document, and as you grow and evolve, so too will your plan.

One thing is for sure, the transportation industry is constantly changing and evolving. To stay ahead of the competition, it's important to stay informed and stay ahead of industry trends. Whether it's implementing new technology, expanding your network, or exploring new markets, there are always opportunities to grow and improve.

So, with that in mind, we wish you all the best on your journey. May your business be successful, and may you find fulfillment in all that you do. With the right attitude and a commitment to excellence, the sky's the limit!

Best of luck on your journey!

In conclusion, we hope that this book has provided you with valuable insights and information to help you navigate the transportation industry with confidence. From strategic planning to financial management, from marketing and branding to human resources, we have covered a wide range of topics to help you build a successful transportation business.

We wish you all the best in your business endeavors and hope that you find success and fulfillment in your work. Remember to stay focused, stay committed, and never stop learning and growing. The transportation industry is constantly changing, and the more you learn and grow, the better equipped you will be to succeed.

So with all the best wishes and success, we say goodbye and look forward to hearing about your continued success in the future. Keep moving forward, and never stop reaching for the stars!